Careful Not to Startle the Yaks

Tanka, Tanka Sequences, and Tanka Prose

Bob Lucky

Copyright© 2025 Bob Lucky
ISBN: 978-93-6354-017-0

First Edition: 2025
Rs. 200/-

Cyberwit.net
HIG 45 Kaushambi Kunj, Kalindipuram
Allahabad - 211011 (U.P.) India
http://www.cyberwit.net
Tel: +(91) 9415091004
E-mail: info@cyberwit.net

No part of this book may be reproduced or transmitted in any form or by
any means, electronic, mechanical, photocopying, or otherwise, without
the express written consent of Bob Lucky.

Printed at Repro India Limited.

For **Gavin,**

who knows what I'm talking about when I talk about bebinca, bibingka, and lapis legit

Preface

It's impossible not to acknowledge Denis Garrison and Michael McClintock of *Modern English Tanka*, editors who had a profound influence on me as a writer, not least because they seemed to like my tanka. Of course, Sanford Goldstein's work with tanka sequences and strings was an inspiration, as was translator Carl Sesar's *Takuboku: Poems to Eat*, which was, fittingly, a gift from food writer John Thorne. Later, though I had written a few sequences, Marilyn Hazelton of *Red Lights* was an influence, spotting sequences in my submissions of individual tanka that I hadn't seen. And, of course, where would tanka prose in general be without Jeffrey Woodward's championing of the form in *The Tanka Prose Anthology* and the journal *Modern Haibun & Tanka Prose*?

As soon as one starts thanking people, there is the risk of leaving someone out, which I don't want to do. M Kei of *Atlas Poetica*, Beverley George of *Eucalypt*, Claire Everett of *Skylark* were also encouraging editors. There were others. I would like to thank them and everyone who's encouraged the appreciation of tanka. And I would be remiss not to bow to the many wonderful writers of the form. The list of journals in the acknowledgements should indicate the scope of my gratitude.

I stopped writing tanka about a year before the Covid pandemic, but I've begun to think in 'five lines down' again and peck at the keyboard now and then. My renewed interest led me back to my earlier work. I've written a lot of tanka over the years, too much for a lazy person like me to deal with. What you have here are the collected sequences, selected individual tanka, and a selection of the shorter tanka prose.

I've made a few edits. It seems I was overly fond of em-dashes in my youth.

Bob Lucky

Viana do Castelo, Portugal

Contents

Duck Tongues, Selected Tanka

I'm trying to see
the point of staying —
if I sit
just so   the moon
floats in my tea

slicing off the crown
cutting out the eyes
pineapple vendor —
she points the knife at me
and names her price

this morning,
not wanting to think
the honeymoon's over,
I shake the milk bottle
and the lid flies off again

golden mangos
hang from every tree —
temptations
I take just a few
as they go quickly

on my street
dogs and cats call a truce
at night
I drop rotten mangos
back into my neighbor's yard

everyone goes on
about the sun and the surf
paradise
all I remember is the grit
of sand in my hot dog

heatwave
the last bunch of cilantro
wilted
I drag myself home
to an ungarnished supper

Chinese New Year
a slurped noodle
in my face
the omens I seek
never find me

a sudden craving
for Sapporo ramen
nostalgia
all the postcards I sent home
in the bottom of a drawer

the lotus' beauty
is not for me
deep down
I crave the root
tempura style

nothingness
begins where it ends…
I ponder
an empty bag
of donut holes

laughter
and the smell of grilled meat
on the wind
no more the bleating
of the neighbor's goat

nothing is
as it appears to be
so it appears
these greasy fries
aren't making me fat

the geography
of good and bad luck
superstition
this year no better or worse
for not eating black-eyed peas

on my own
in the night market
I haggle
over the price of dried fish
just for the conversation

at the market
a bowl of blood
on the table
the turtle's legs paddle air
as the monger cuts away

on the bus
to Hangzhou Station
no one but me
stares at the old man
slurping dumplings

killing time
over a bowl of soup
I watch the vendor
knead and stretch dough
filling his night with noodles

in a friend's cafe
we sample the chef's latest
pickled day lilies
the conversation turns
to the belt-tightening times

not hungry
until I smell the bacon,
not thirsty
until I taste the wine,
not much at all until…

this is the last time
I will ever write about
a raspberry tart
they're never as good
as I think they should be

the jackfruit seller
who ripped me off yesterday
smiles
and tries to rip me off
for a little less today

aging is not
without distractions —
balancing
bags of frozen vegetables
on arthritic knees

at the sushi bar
the drunk drones on about
one that got away
with a wave of his chopsticks
he sends sashimi flying

at a *taquería*
near my parents' house
an old man
asks in Spanish
for an English menu

at the gate
to the Temple of Literature
I turn back
losing myself in the steam
from a bowl of rice noodles

dipping
a stiff flatbread
into cold lentils —
for this and the mountain view
I've walked all morning

the carnage
of pomegranate
for dessert
we sit in silence
popping seeds into our mouths

antique teapots
line the walls in her house
the collector
offers me a cup
of instant coffee

the dining room
banked by steam trays
and shiny ladles
fishing in the soup tureen
for the rumored shrimp

having a pint
at The Hospital Arms
with my son —
in lieu of conversation
we read Spike Milligan

splitting
a club sandwich
at the cafe
the odd feeling of knowing
I can't afford to live long

the scraping
sound of a spoon on plastic
my father
continues to eat the yogurt
he finished earlier

I call my father
on his eightieth birthday
after all these years
he tells me how much he loves
honey on frozen waffles

passing through
the cereal aisle
I can't remember
what it was
my mother used to like

chopping onions
my grandmother's knife
still sharp
the sound of her voice
when the blade hits the board

a sugar shortage
is announced in the papers —
everyday I stop
to scan the shelves
and imagine bitterness

slowly drinking
a cup of fragrant oolong
I hope to die
before that day we go
to war over water

dressed in black
widows sit around the table
shelling peas
all afternoon
till the end of time

seagulls gather
at the fish and chips wagon
lunch hour
tourists don't see the good luck
in being shat upon

one avocado
in a bowl of mangos
and bananas —
no matter how I fit in
I'm always out of place

the heart
is the muscle
I pulled
slowly stirring sugar
into my bitter cup

sucking
the juice out of
passion fruit
I would stand here
all day if I could

past time
to say goodbye, the rain
keeps falling —
surely these tea leaves
hold another cup

in the labyrinth
of middle age
walking on eggshells—
instead of make-up sex
we share an omelet

I watch you dress
in the light of a dim bulb —
how was I
to know the meaning of love
is not the same in all rooms

after dinner
the silence thickens —
the disagreement
over how to reheat risotto
still simmering

palm fronds
rattle in the breeze —
the conversation
we think we're having
ended a while ago

mid-sentence
she wanders off talking
to herself —
it doesn't really matter
but it was my sentence

disagreement
over *Midnight in Paris*
when was it
we started to talk about
the past more than the future

prayer flags
color the breeze
conversations
we might have had
seem possible again

reading
between the lines
of your letter
I feel the man I was
falling through the gaps

tonight
she made me hash browns
and fried eggs
because she loves me, I think
what else could it be

we never had
a song we called
our own —
now everyone I hear
could be the one

once
I came home early
and caught you
singing a song I wrote —
it never happened again

passing the window
of a lingerie shop
she stops to explain
tight bras and breast cancer
and my spirits droop

watching old women
kiss the out-held cross
I turn to you
and shudder to think of
all the things we've kissed

when we were young
we pushed twin beds together —
budget hotel
across the emptiness
our hands touch goodnight

dry champagne
and some nibbles
quiet anniversary
the big hunk of stinky cheese
almost gone

it annoys me
how you want to share
dessert
I wish you were here
to bug me about this mango

I'll call you
by another name and sleep
on the other side —
you won't be you
and I won't be me

sliding my feet
into her furry slippers
Valentine's Day
the omelet I promised
and a pot of oolong

you pour me
another cup of tea —
the cactus
on the patio
still hasn't bloomed

another attempt
to fix the crack in the tile —
from this angle
what separates us
keeps us together

dreaming
impervious to
reality
uncrackable pistachios
pile up between us

side by side
her notepad and mine
retirement plans
the wobble
in the café table

sycamore leaves
turn in a warm breeze
remembering
that afternoon we planned
to sail around the world

steam clouds
the kitchen window —
long marriage
making perfect congee
with leftover rice

Lost in Language and Hunger: The Collected Sequences

Towards a Narrative Theory

today
I have to read
Madame Bovary
craving *teurgole*
on this gloomy Sunday

the boy
wants to marry the girl,
that's not the story
I'm here to tell you
it's just fabula

my teenaged son
walks ten paces ahead
or ten behind —
every conversation
a shout through space and time

unable to read
I point to a picture
on the menu
that soothing bowl of noodles
in a broth too hot to eat

reading
narrative theory
I fall asleep
in my dreams I find
embedded dreams

Chinese Lessons

local hair salon
she asks in English if I
speak Chinese
not well, I say in Chinese
cutting the air with finger-scissors

seven million souls
knocking about this city
down by the lake
I see everyone I know
trying to be alone too

hoping the thieves
don't have time to break in
a new bike
I've left on the bubble wrap
but use a chain as well

muggy evening
I envy old Chinese men
who pull up their shirts
where they please
and fan their pot bellies

the duck tongues
are passed my way
I nibble slowly
wondering if I'll ever
say what I want in Chinese

The Seven Essentials
  after a Chinese proverb

near the gardens
that line the river bank
an old man
lifts a bundle of firewood
onto his hunched back

no customers
in her shop, the vendor
rakes the rice
into perfect mounds
that might be found in heaven

on the curb
a woman drizzles oil
on a black griddle —
I join the huddled hungry
and wait for my flatbread

down the aisles
of a Chinese grocery
I scan the shelves —
there among five kilo bags
of msg, a tiny box of salt

two years in China
and I'm still afraid to try
the soy sauce
the old woman ladles
from a fifty-gallon drum

butchering Chinese
in an upscale restaurant,
we go through waiters
until one understands
our need for some vinegar

in Longjing village
the Dragon Well tea harvest
has begun
in shops all over town
last year's tea is a bargain

Chinese Spring

Beijing spring day
grows cold and dark, a throwback
to winter gloom —
beneath an unlit street lamp
a boy sits on his soccer ball

mindful
of the uneven steps
along the Great Wall
not sure if the icy blast
is coming in or going out

returning
to work in Hangzhou —
outside my window
purple magnolia blossoms
replaced by dusty bulbuls

spring fever
could be smog induced
three students out sick
the day I give a test
on industrialization

Sunday morning stroll
in the park I drift through
pink skies
a forest of cherry trees
planted too close together

wedding shoot
just before dusk at lakeside
the red gown
of one young bride-to-be
catches the last of the light

tired of the crowds
the rudeness born of
self-preservation
I slip into Starbucks
and nurse a macchiato

piles of books to pack
piles to sale or give away —
students ask me why
I'm going to Africa
or where it is exactly

again tonight
the sudden crash
of rain —
for a brief moment I stop
sucking the mango pit

my last Chinese spring
part of me wants to see it all —
I hang out
with the part that is content
to slurp a bowl of noodles

A Sunday in Addis

the watchman
doubles as our gardener —
what possesses him
to grow a wall of roses
beautiful enough to steal

walking the dog
looking up at circling hawks
I'm stopped
by a little girl who smiles
and gives me her balloon

Sunday afternoon
the crowd at the sidewalk cafe
lost in the news —
across the street two boys
wrestle a bull to a halt

our Muslim cook
has discovered the meaning
of Chanukah —
it's a miracle
we don't get latkes tonight

on the verandah
a pot of glowing coals
between us
the half moon and silence
all there is to talk about

the coolness
of the African highlands
an eternity
waiting for the water
to boil for tea

darkness
lost among the stars
once again
we listen for hyenas
until we fall asleep

Roman Holiday

the older I get
the less I care
about ruins
all the marble penises
lopped off

the sounds
of a commuter tram
and my wife's breathing —
the name of this wine different
every time I drink it

looking out
on the Spanish Steps
from Keats's room
so glad to be this old
and still able to suffer

Off La Rambla

> "No hi ha cap ciutat lletja,
> cap home ni cap dona
> tan miserables que no puguem ser
> tu i jo en aquesta història d'amor."
> — *Joan Margarit*

in Barcelona
reading Bolaño's poetry
I wonder
if the statue of Columbus
is pointing the wrong way

my old friend
stands in the kitchen and toasts
the new year
goodbye grilled tiger prawns
hello rabbit paella

live musicians
keep the crowds moving
in Parc Grüell
the tiled lizard frozen
in a million photos

the parade
passes Plaça de Catalunya —
night of the three kings
Spain's new antismoking law
turns sidewalks into lounges

the crowd three deep
behind barstools at El Quim
when we find two spots
we stare at the menu board
lost in language and hunger

tense, quiet morning
after coffee and croissants
we walk for miles —
finally I have to point out
the hotel's the other way

A Turn Around Central Mongolia

four hours
in a Russian saddle
black and blue
gathering clouds darken
the Mongolian sky

inside the *ger*
the camel-dung fire glows
I crouch outside
and watch the snowflakes
land on my arm and melt

the singer
demonstrates the four types
of throat singing —
as hard as I try
I can't suppress a cough

careful
not to startle the yaks
I keep my flashlight
steady on the path
that leads to the outhouse

Old Man Rock
looks like a puffed-up toad
to me
a magpie's white breast
the only cloud in the sky

if I had not
been born in the century
of Freud
would the path through the outcrop
look like a vagina

on the shore
of Great White Lake
people watch sunset —
I turn my back and catch
the full moon rising

after a week
without toilet or shower
a kind of joy
back in the Soviet gray
of Ulaanbaatar

A Quiet Evening

the quiet
of evening slips
into the garden
one by one I lose
count of the birds

looking deep
into the sky
I see
how far away
I've drifted

In the distance
the rattle of an empty
delivery truck —
alone in bed thinking
I didn't pay my dues

Suspended Between Hanging On and Letting Go

the silence
that fills the night
weighs on me
across the freeway
the moon just out of reach

burning all
my grad school papers
in the fireplace
the glowing zigzags
of melting staples

once a week
the women gather for
a stitch and bitch
upstairs with a glass of wine
I count my blessings

Almost Asleep

burying
my feet
beneath the sand
I disinter
a cigarette butt

waves
whisper to the sand —
almost asleep
my dreams float
between day and night

for a year now
when I look
out to sea
I'm not sure
what I'm looking for

the man
who never says
good morning
I see him at the café
signing to a friend

call to prayer
drowns out
our conversation
despite my reservations
it appears god is merciful

Aging

coolness
of a November
twilight
waves break softly
upon the shore

the rigging
on a dry-docked boat
clatters in the wind —
the fluttering of my dream
to sail around the world

faded warning sign
at the end of the pier
a fisherman
casts his line
as far as he can

the sand
pits my soul —
always something
on the beach
that shouldn't be there

digging deep
to touch my toes
how flexible
one must be to fit
into a coffin

Fairly Certain

willing now
to pray…
but
the words don't come
and the knees won't bend

over a lunch
of spring water and salad
still hungry
for a solution that might
include a burger and a beer

beyond the sound
of palms jostling each other
in the breeze
the sound of the surf
slapping the shore

the cursive notes
in my grandfather's Bible —
with a finger
I trace his thoughts
in a language I can't read

fairly certain
I'll be dead before
the end of the world
what do I say to my son
who probably won't be

Kith & Kin

clearing out
the old homestead
empty birdcage
grandpa teaches me
to whistle again

cold snap
the warmth of father's gloves
now mine
the hand that never
reached out

without a word
slowing our pace
to catch sunset
a firefly's flash
in the silence

spring evening
all the windows open
I hear America
singing full-throated
in the neighbor's bedroom

late spring
the whir of weed whackers
my nap's soundtrack
no matter the dream
I side with the weeds

A Deep Breath

reading old recipes
the way grandma could make
so much of so little —
reorganizing the pantry
by expiration dates

crows
dapple the sky
in the park
a chain of caws
linking the trees

this morning
a bumper crop of strange dreams —
I send an email
to all my dead friends
just to see

every year
I think of doing without
the candles —
taking a deep breath,
wishing you were here again

scraping burnt bits
off my morning toast. . .
grandfather
used to burn his toast
so carefully

All Weather Is Good, a Complete Fiction

this year
we planned
to reminisce
but can't agree on
where we've been

imagining
a life without her
an empty glass
waiting to be filled
and emptied

picking
at the grilled fish for two
trial separation
but not yet at the stage
where we split the check

driving home
through the storm passing
through the world
I'm passing through
alone

wishing
I knew which star
to wish upon…
the neighbors banging away
in the apartment upstairs

Another Afternoon

the fact
that we are doomed
no matter what
another afternoon
killing time in a café

in the café
listening to an old man
tell his tale —
we've all heard it before
but every time it's louder

the bay
a tangle of kitesurfers
in the afternoon
I walk along the shore
to unravel my life

all the pains
I have become
symptoms
every step going up
takes me down

my love
for everyone tested
today
I muster just enough
pity to like myself

A Scribbled Map, Selected Shorter Tanka Prose

Death in the Afternoon

The way the light from the setting sun comes through the glass door and spills across the marble floor of the lobby would be comfort enough if not for the body of a dead fly ripping into the light and lying in the puddle of its shadow. I sweep it aside with my shoe before the crowd behind me tramples it underfoot.

sinking lower
into the worn sofa —
doctor's waiting room
the face of a clock reflected
in the TV's dark screen

Resurrection

One day last winter, I came home from work and there he was,
my imaginary friend, curled up in a corner of the living room, like
a hunger artist. I swept him up and put him in the compost bin.
There was no point in getting the authorities involved. None of
my answers would've matched their questions.

bumper crop
of tomatoes this year —
my neighbor
filling her basket
calls it a miracle

Diagnosis

Sitting in the clinic waiting for results. The list of things the doctor wants to rule out is enough to make me ill. I think of writing a letter to my wife and son in case I don't come out of this alive. "If I should die" I begin, but that's the beginning of every story, and the end.

a scribbled map
in my notebook
the stars
at the end of the road
pointing every which way

Anticipating Grief

I wake into
an afternoon steeped in dreams
something like Wagner
pumped out of speakers hidden
in bushes, behind mirrors

Far away my father kicks off his covers and wonders where he
is, sees people who aren't there, asks the nurses as they move
him back into bed what kind of religion this is. Here I argue with
my son about grades, with my wife about money, with myself
about love. When everyone's in bed, I search online for cheap
flights.

On How to Write an Obituary

I want to thank everyone for coming tonight, for taking part in Muddy Creek Community College's Continuing Education course "How to Write an Obituary." It pleases me to see a few young people here. So many times it's those of us of more mature years who enroll in this course, with one eye, our good one, on another offering, Memoir Writing, which I will teach in the spring, the former instructor, Mrs. Sogren, having passed on to that great classroom in the sky. The simple fact is, death will always be with us; an enterprising young man or woman couldn't go wrong to contemplate a rewarding career as a journalist specializing in, well, death, a career as an obituarist. It has a certain ring, you must admit, even if it doesn't trip lightly off this old swollen tongue. Please carefully look over the syllabus I am passing out to you now. This course meets once a week for the next three weeks, by which time you should be prepared to write a publishable obituary, yours or someone else's dear to you. Tonight we are going to examine the golden rule of obituary writing: Make sure the person is dead before you publish.

idling hearse
the driver checks
his watch
the church bells not adjusted
for daylight saving time

A Lesson in Something

1.
warm night
the clink of ice
in my glass
remembering the glint
of grandpa's ice pick

My grandfather wakes me long before sunrise. We eat breakfast
in silence and then load the tools into the bed of the pickup. At
the icehouse, he works large blocks of ice into his water coolers.
I watch as if I'm learning something.

2.

Up late after finishing a project for work, I stare at a photo of my
father. It's been two months since he died and I still haven't
cried. Last night I dreamt about him for the first time. All he said
was *shut up*.

stepping out
to admire the moon —
in the shadows
my own dog barks at me
until I call her name

Ignoring Dylan Thomas Sometimes, Sometimes Not

A hip and a shoulder on opposite sides are tightening up, giving me a sort of rolling gait. I stumble into the night splotchy-skinned, the hair on my arms thicker than on my head. Muscle is turning inexorably into flab, except for the heart, which is doubtless hardening with the arteries. My eyes grow dimmer every day, and yet when I see you sleeping there, a strand of hair across your face, the nightgown sliding off your shoulder, I want to hold on a little longer.

late autumn
toppling into a pile
of leaves —
the fragrance of earth
deep in my lungs

Trying to Ignore Mortality by Using the Second Person Pronoun Until the End

At the entrance to Petra you're struck by the smell of horse manure, but as you're still reeling from the shock of the entry fee, you stumble past the gauntlet of horse and carriage guides toward the Siq. A few hours later you realize the guides all bear a resemblance to Johnny Depp in *Pirates of the Caribbean* and speak English like Chico Marx. And no matter how fat and tired and old you are, you're going to walk all the way back and have an ice cream cone at Mövenpick.

the empty tombs
of Nabatean kings —
in the dim light
nothing but graffiti
and my nagging cough

The Candidate

chance of rain
the morning after
a televised debate —
just another promise
never fulfilled

In the waiting room, my mother quietly waits for her name to be called. There are a few other patients waiting as well. The sound on the TV is off. I'm watching a Viagra commercial and imagining the look on that man's face when he walks awkwardly into the clinic, with his four-hour erection. "Who was that politician," my mother blurts out, "who couldn't get it up?"

On My Way, Not Exactly What Dr. Seuss Had in Mind

Looking down Rua da Constituição, I can see the Atlantic Ocean
in the distance. I could walk there if I made a sinistrad cut
toward Avenida da Boavista and turned right. A couple of hours
at most. I'm not sure what I would do there, but once there, I
would have to walk back, and not wanting to retrace my steps,
I'd probably walk south along the coast to the mouth of the
Douro River and then trek uphill on a diagonal to Serralves Park,
where, taking advantage of the senior discount, I'd wander
through the park admiring the garden and some of the sculptures
and stop for an espresso at the Casa da Chá, which, despite its
name doesn't give tea a good name. At that point, my right foot,
slightly larger than my left foot and squeezed into its shoe, would
be bothering me, and I'd have to decide whether to take a taxi or
limp home. However, today I'm on my way to an acupuncture
appointment.

all the places
I could drag myself
retirement blues
an old map coming apart
at the seams

In Lieu of a Prayer I Drink a Toast to Chance

I know how chance works, that every time I step into a plane the
odds of going down in flames are always the same no matter
how often I fly. 36,000 feet in the air, I look out the window and
see Jeddah lit up like…. I want to say a Christmas tree.

safe from jumping cows
the full moon floats in darkness —
inside the plane
the rattle of the drinks cart
brings me back to earth

Jetlag

Throughout the night, I listen to the sound of drawers opening and closing, the creaking of doors, rattle of cutlery, murmur of television commercials, unzipping and zipping of suitcases. At some point, I decide to pretend to be asleep. My dreams aren't real.

sunlight
burning through
the fog —
her side of the bed
still made

Overlapping Realities at Breakfast
Siem Reap, Cambodia

Along the edge of the jungle orange-clad monks carry bowls
filled with a variety of cooked vegetables, fresh fruit, heaps of
steamed rice, and cooked rice in banana leaves back to their *wat*.
The procession slowly disappears into the green foliage like a
snake, a meandering river, an old steam train, a hungry caterpillar,
a dream…dragging my thoughts behind it.

in the muggy dawn
the waiter brings two eggs
sunny side up —
the guidebook fails to mention
the beggar at my table

A Fish Tale

a kingfisher lights
on a branch overhanging
Phewa Lake —
the reflection of mountains
shattered by feathers

Walking around Pokhara, my wife and I are struck by how many people are carrying fish, two or three on a line, a plastic bag full. Chalk sketches of fish appear on menu boards. "Fish Fry" is the special of the day regardless of the cuisine. After a lakeside lunch at Mike's Restaurant, my wife asks the waiter about the fish. "Half price on Friday," he says, refilling my coffee.

Kashmir

My friend and I ride horses up a mountain until a storm heading
our way crests a ridge. The guide has us dismount, slaps the
horses on their rumps, and says follow me. We run down the
mountain and through a forest. "*Jaldi! Jaldi!*" The guide shouts.
We're going as fast as we can, bumping into and off trees,
tripping over roots and stones. One must always trust the guide in
emergencies, and this is an emergency — we are being chased
down the mountain by the storm, and running out of breath and
the will to live. "*Aloo! Aloo!*" The guide shouts in what seems
like alarm. At that point, I feel I'm going to die anyway so the
threat of trampling some potato patch isn't a real concern. 30
years later, reminiscing in the dim bar of a Delhi hotel, my friend
says to me, "You do know that the guide was shouting *bhaloo*,
bear, not *aloo*?"

another order
of potato chaat
growing cold
the story that could've been
all these years

Instead of Reading *Hamlet* on a Beach in Thailand

It's tempting on this secluded beach to pick up a coconut, gaze into its eyes and speak to it. Yesterday, driving down the muddy rut the road has become in the rainy season, I waved at a macaque that was sitting on a rock at the edge of the jungle. It was an instinctual gesture, one primate to another. The macaque just stared at me and scratched its belly.

ghost crabs
scurry over the hot sand
ahead of the surf —
I swim out and let
the sea wash me ashore

Holiday Routine

Occasionally I look up from Franz Kafka's diaries to locate my
wife's snorkel.

wetsuits drying
on beachside balconies
afternoon glare
the head on my beer
slowly disappearing

Another Bad Love Poem

"Love: an old man with a broken wrist, his white beard glimmer-
ing in the moonlight."
 – Peter Johnson, "The Worst Love Poem Ever Written"

Iceland. On a deck at the Blue Lagoon, I slip. My left wrist
trembles in the air like a question mark. A crowd gathers. The
staff confers, every move calculated to thwart a lawsuit. The
rest of the day: ambulances, hospitals, and generous doses of
morphine. The sun is still up when I expect moon in the sky. An
EMT tells me how he likes to go shopping in Atlanta. I'm not
much of a shopper so the conversation dies. Then a doctor pulls
on my wrist until he can pull no more. My wife huddles with a
bunch of white coats, and I think I love you, babe. I may have
said it.

midnight sun
riding a morphine wave
into darkness —
flowers that don't exist
blossom in my dreams

Another Starry Night

Taking a walk to cool off, I wish I could get my hands on what-
ever absinthe van Gogh was drinking. The stars don't twinkle or
swirl tonight. They're like pinpricks in a blackout curtain.

spat
with my wife —
too old
to volunteer
for the Mar's trip

The World Is Full of Heroes

After every glass of beer, Ron claims someone else to be his
hero. I notice the beer garden is carpeted in fallen jacaranda
blossoms, but it's not an observation that fits neatly into the
conversation. As the night darkens our view, I turn to him and
ask if I could be his hero. "Why not?" he mumbles. "Anyone
who does what I ought to do but don't is a hero to me." I ask
what I've done to become his hero. "Could you get me another
beer?" he asks.

moonlight puddles
around green plastic tables —
draining my glass
a hole in the Big Dipper
almost visible

Eve, the Orchard Years

The apples that don't fall far from the tree get picked, packed, shipped, sliced, and crammed into lunch boxes thousands of miles away or just rot on the ground with all the other fallen apples. Adam brews some good cider, but he doesn't like to share it. During the harvest season, the kids bring their kids to help. No one talks about the good old days anymore.

paradise
the birds and the bees
at it again…
a slithering ripple
beneath fallen apple blossoms

Wise Guy

without a sound
moonlight slips into the house —
a lifetime
spent trying to fit in
where I don't belong

"If you were looking for the truth, where would you start?" my partner asked. As an apprentice burglar, I suspected I was being tested. Perhaps truth was slang for treasure. I shrugged to convey both my ignorance and my admiration for the profundity of the question. We went into the bathroom and he flipped through a tattered copy of Bill Peet's *No Such Things* and checked to see if the dental floss was scented. In the bedroom he nicked a few jewels out of habit. "What do you think?" he asked. I shrugged again, this time to give the impression I was thinking the same thing he was thinking. We went into the kitchen and he pulled a bread knife out of a drawer and ran a finger, one of mine to be exact, over the heel. I didn't say anything because I thought this might be some sort of burglars' blood brother ritual. He laid the knife on the counter and said, "Let's go. We've found it." "Found what?" I asked. "The truth." I looked at my finger and was about to ask when he said, "Yes, that's your cut."

Preface to Canto IV of *The Three Virgins of Rosenberg, Texas*

In this canto the poet laments his inability to find the virgins. He curses God for hiding them so perfectly that the virgins themselves may have no clue as to who they are. Through a variety of rhetorical questions, the poet wrestles with his failure. Anthypophoria is employed to great effect — "Is virginity the Lord's sleight of hand?/Invisible it is from where I stand." Likewise is epiplexis — "Have you no sympathy for the virgins?" he asks the people of the town. Before the poet retires to a Mexican restaurant for an enchilada plate, the focus of Canto V, he asks an erotetic question: "Do I not look like a man who could spot/A virgin or three in a parking lot?"

people pretending
to remember each other
high school reunion
my nametag upside down
so I don't forget who I was

Kitchen Magic

dinner party
grinding grains of paradise
for groundnut soup —
the plumber fixing the sink
asks, what's that smell

The cheapest way to renovate a kitchen is to buy a cookbook. But it must be about a cuisine unfamiliar, exotic to you, Ghanaian, for example. Preferably in a language you'll have to learn. Twi is a challenge for the tone deaf but at least it's written in the Roman alphabet. Next, there's the cost of a round-trip ticket to Accra, and accommodations and expenses for a couple weeks. Spend time in Makola Market shopping for ingredients, especially spices and jars of shito. Eat a lot. Try tuo zaafi, which uses dawadawa and ayoyo leaves; fufu and goat light soup; and red-red if you're vegetarian. Fly home with stuffed suitcases and invite your friends over for a Ghanaian feast. They won't notice how out-of-date your split-pea green fridge is or the old grease stains on the wall behind the stove. No one will care the counter tops are cracked. It may cost you, but that's the cheapest way to renovate a kitchen.

Ethnographic Vignette #1

The anthropologists showed the villagers a film of village life and asked them what they saw. They all saw a chicken. The anthropologists were amazed, confused. They couldn't recall seeing a chicken, so they watched the film again and in one scene spied a chicken in the bottom right corner, a blur of a chicken, a cameo appearance. There are many ways to be human, they concluded. Some people don't know how to watch a film.

clouds
moonlit from above
overnight flight
all my dreams
silent movies

Ethnographic Vignette #2

afternoon glare
I follow the shade
across the street
an hourglass on its side
in a pawnshop window

In the 1950s, Bedouin came out of the desert to be plowed down by the cars in Morocco's growing cities. Anthropologists were curious how space and time are calculated, how the cultural measurement of speed is made. It turns out the Bedouin were on camel time: nothing could move faster than a camel (except, of course, a car, which was the point of the study). It may seem obvious to us now, but it took many dead Bedouin to confirm that what we don't know can kill us, even if we look both ways when we cross the street.

The Problem with Time

Forever was a long time ago.

where the moon
drifts across the river
I cast a line —
there is no ideal bait
for the one that got away

Acknowledgments

Thanks are due to the editors and publishers of the following journals and anthologies in which these poems previously appeared:

3 Lights Gallery, A Hundred Gourds, American Tanka, Among the Lilies, Atlas Poetica, bottle rockets, Bright Stars, Contemporary Haibun Online, Chrysanthemum, Drifting Sands Haibun, Eucalypt, Failed Haiku, Fire Pearls 2, Gusts, Haibun Today, KYSO, MacQueen's Quarterly, Magnapoets, Modern English Tanka, Moonset, Notes from the Gean, Presence, Prune Juice, Red Lights, Ribbons, Simply Haiku, Skylark, Stylus Poetry Journal, Tanka Prose Anthology, White Lotus.

www.ingramcontent.com/pod-product-compliance
Lightning Source LLC
LaVergne TN
LVHW051507170726
843492LV00002B/834